Some Poems

Also by John Seed

Spaces In (Pig Press, Newcastle-upon-Tyne 1977)
History Labour Night. Fire & Sleet & Candlelight (Pig Press, Durham 1984)
Transit Depots (Ship of Fools, London 1993)
Interior in the Open Air (Reality Street, London 1993)
Divided into One (Poetical Histories, Cambridge 2003)
New & Collected Poems (Shearsman, Exeter 2005)
Pictures from Mayhew: London 1850 (Shearsman, Exeter 2005)
That Barrikins: Pictures from Mayhew II (Shearsman, Exeter, 2007)
Manchester: August 16th & 17th 1819 (Intercapillary Editions, London 2013)

Some Poems

2006–2013

John Seed

Gratton Street Irregulars

First published in the United Kingdom in 2014 by
Gratton Street Irregulars
1 Gratton Street
Cheltenham
GL50 2AT

and distributed by
Shearsman Books Ltd
50 Westons Hill Drive
Emersons Green
Bristol
BS16 7DF

ISBN 978-1-84861-373-7

ACKNOWLEDGEMENTS
A few of these poems have appeared in *Great Works*,
Intercapillary Space, Onedit and Shadow Train—and possibly elsewhere.
Thanks to hard-working editors Tim Atkins, Edmund Hardy,
Peter Philpott and Ian Seed.

Obits of the day

From dark to twilight and dark again

Hiss of tyres along tree-lined avenues

Suburban grids surveillance logs

Beech leaves missing-persons reports

London's icy shimmer of lights

Whispers and rumours

Watery surfaces

Rain a few seconds ago

Roehampton Lane

I

*From Genthe's Photographs of San
Francisco's Old Chinatown 1895–1906*

1

Each green stalk

a paper ring

on a bed

of pebbles white

narcissus in clay

pots icy slivers

of sunlight on

an upturned box

2

Wrapped in a

blanket drawing on

a long pipe

his table display

of used teapots

cloth tassels

wire bird-cage

a kitten watches

3

Too old for
hard labour the
pipe-bowl mender
bathed in sunlight
wire-rim spectacles
tools on a
sack on a
doorstep his workshop

4

Slave girl daughter
of Tien-hou
head down against
the cold hurrying
shadow a wintry
moment on the
corner kerbstone by
the Globe Hotel

Far away on the cold mountain
A stone path slants up among
White clouds people have their homes
Half-hidden I wait for a
While loving the woods in the
Evening frozen leaves each leaf singular
Redder than any spring flower autumn

April spent

May too

so soon

how many more spring mornings evenings…

smoky wisp of a life

dim towers loom out of the misty rain

Drift of dead leaves

piled against a closed gate

no footprints in grass grown wild

suddenly an old man . . .

is this hard wind blowing all the way to T'ai-shan

white clouds drift there without end

1

Mist veils the cold
Stream moonlight the sand
Mooring in the shadow
Of a river-tavern as
Empires collapse
Golden-lantern girls
Dance to no tune

2

Solitary in company shadow
awake half the night red
glow of dawn breaking
haze on the river trust
to the current a boat
moored waiting

3

Stories of passion sweet dust
Chill water indifferent lines
Shadows hills clouds islands
Facing West into a great flood
Of light at sunset when
Birds call in the still
Air leaves are falling like
Like a girl's robe long ago

4

Drifting past the window outside
First flurries of snow bright
Particles at dusk falling I'm
Inside afloat hugging the duvet
Half-asleep a boat adrift
Hazy autumn river not far
From trouble but far enough

II

and there she was
Clio   a muse
naked
descending the stairs in
autumn lighting
with a parchment scroll
stylus or
set of tablets
infinity lip tint and smile

trampers arrive in twilight
arc of mist air chill
ragged and tanned
and shelter without money

hawkers sturdy beggars footpads
on the prowl a young thief narrated
dog-carts wandering the counties
selling brooms lines door-mats

travel for scraps enough
you get for a kerchief
seeking markets
for their labour some London

dead dogs

offal from slaughter-houses entrails of animals

pavement dirt stable dung night soil

bodies of murdered

evacuations of the human

washed into the Thames and the tide

washes it back again the

water we use is   we drink

a solution of our own faeces

stump
bedsteads

half room
time with curtain

motes lighted
candle placed

neck an empty bottle
night's merriment

which tales
miseries are

calculate disturbing forces
obstruction's rough palms
surplus population in any parish
chargeable becomes removable
audits the last place wanted

neighbouring under peril sent
idle famished disorderly punishable
vagrants vagabonds treadmill rents
removed deleted transported
bid adieu St Giles a season

fear gallows before their eyes
higher walks   straws floating
on tides destiny races Greenwich fair
unlucky one said I'm always

nabbed on Friday
last time catched Monday
leery lads first thing out of prison
get kerchief get dinner

profits but merry enough
what he is born to again
reckless and dogged
sentences   impossible to escape

Hanged at Tyburn
Cut down still breathing
Disembowelled headed
Quarters set on the city gates the
Old Roman road from Oxford
Deep hollow full of sloughs
Right and left diverging cross-streets
Rusting car-bodies propped on bricks
Here and there a ragged house
Living place of cut-throats
People swept into dark corners I
Went in dread the whole way

May 1804 Wednesday
morning about 5 o'clock
a young woman (17)
left her work
at the Smyrna Coffee-house St. James's Street
walked through the Palace
and into the Park
and into the bason
and was seen no more

till 7 o'clock
when her lifeless body was taken out

and nothing found in her pockets
except some halfpence
wrapped in white paper
on which was written
'Fanny White Lambeth'

vagrant acts helpless

suffered to wander about
flocked to its shores
from the land of winter wintry audits
on coal vessels a return cargo
thrust on shore at night
in obscure parts of the
river exhausted faint making for
nowhere in great bitterness of soul
without stockings shirts shoes

famished prison has no terrors
stone-yard retreat from cold
a heap of stones
broken the previous day

twilight Acheron the winter fields

asleep in

a far cry from

as regards males for each entire day of detention
the breaking of seven cwt. of stones or other such quantity
not less than five cwt. nor more than thirteen cwt.
as the Guardians having regard to the nature of the stone may
       prescribe
the stone shall be broken to such a size
as the Guardians having regard to the nature thereof may
       prescribe
or the picking of four pounds of unbeaten or eight pounds of
       beaten oakum
or nine hours work in digging or pumping
or cutting wood or grinding corn or

                              heavens end
autumn tramping the counties the Bath Road
night towards refuge lodging anywhere
four ounces of bread ounce of cheese
a man comes to it middle-aged finds it hard
witnesses judges sentences separations
bridewells treadmills County Gaol
houses of refuge House of Correction
silent systems other gaols
expiation it's soon done
postscript sorrow ashes dusk

Terminus god of boundary stones
under Heathrow's flight-paths
erased by the road
new paths with pine needles
altered walking
along the edge of an escarpment

voices I found or imagined

an outside or limit to

III

Massachusetts

1
What now is
was summer
one Sunday Boston harbour's watery dusty gulfs of blue shadow
morning along the wooden jetties
NO LOITERING
2008
in the smoky breeze Atlantic brightness

2
strips of blue
cloud the western sky
glows behind red oaks
tall white Calvinist steeples

Concord pronounced conquered

celestial functionaries of Empire daydreaming
equity leafy
shadows squared-off privet for each
station of the august
twilight temple of the five winds

Till Howdy-Maw

In memory Bill Griffiths

1.

Sea-front right / south

remains on paper

warehouses left

between warehouses Foundry Road

works Entrance

with their backs to the light

Square and school and I'm

here Bill   there

same way the sun revolved

Alfred Street

on the verge of

2

Old poets good

for more than

wandering the roads

a hundred miles

of white cloud

floated out of

the west appearing

vanishing all day

who notices who

else notices heaven

and earth go

about their business

3

Byker Hill and Walker shore

Collier lads for evermore!

Pit-laddie keel-laddie

Cold salt

Waters of the Tyne

Autumn waters of the

Tyne golden

Shadows in the last rays smoking

Till howdy-maw

Chester-le-Street 1955

long as a shadow lasts a
few thousand Fridays ago

granite surfaces turn to mist

great banks of white cloud gone

Miss Duffy Miss Widdrington
Mr Batey in his high office
beyond the clouds busy

opal light soft rain ashes

evenings long since dark

sparks fly up and go out

fifty Novembers gone where

to retrace their steps from
Ropery Lane I remember

market-day queues by Chester Co-op
Doggarts the 94 gone

where they are
still where

the sun will always shine
new blue skies last forever

Imagine a line
imagine it projected
outside the papers

edge windows frame
a road converging
to another obscured

by dark trees
between waymark posts
into shadows quick

footsteps breathing counterpoint
over the same
ground all day

walking across furze
and heath in
windy weather is

where I'd like
to be horizontal
on rough grass

a hilltop between
heaven and earth
smoking rainclouds sweep

north winds gust
off cold fields
hissing among rushes

the rivers edge
wandering alleys rattling
doors windows October

morning a thousand
October mornings wintry
boroughs opal light

Declare

Declare

Geraldine Clarkson

Shearsman Books

First published in the United Kingdom in 2016 by
Shearsman Books, 50 Westons Hill Drive, Emersons Green
BRISTOL BS16 7DF

Shearsman Books Ltd Registered Office
30–31 St. James Place, Mangotsfield, Bristol BS16 9JB
(this address not for correspondence)

www.shearsman.com

ISBN 978-1-84861-506-9

ACKNOWLEDGEMENTS

Thanks are due to the editors of the following journals and publications
in which some of these poems have previously appeared: *Ambit, Magma,
Poetry London, Tears in the Fence, The Poetry Review, The Rialto,* and *Under
the Radar*; the 2014 and 2015 Ware Poetry Competition Anthologies; and,
in particular, *Primers: Volume 1* (Nine Arches Press & The Poetry School).
'T-E-N-G-U' was commissioned by Roddy Lumsden for his BroadCast
series. 'His Wife in the Corner' won the Poetry London competition
2015, 'Brother' won the *Ambit* competition 2015, and 'Afflatus in My
Home Town' won the Ver Poets Prize 2015.

I should like to thank the Arvon and Jerwood Foundations, and
Writers' Centre Norwich, for championing my writing at an early stage.

My personal thanks go to Ahren Warner for his enthusiasm and
advice in helping me to develop and realise this chapbook; to Kathryn
Maris for believing in my work and for her invaluable guidance and
insights; and to all those poets and friends who have promoted and
encouraged my work at various stages, especially David Caddy,
Carol Ann Duffy, Ian Duhig, Carrie Etter, Tony Frazer, Anne-Marie Fyfe,
Eve Grubin, Roddy Lumsden, Glyn Maxwell, Daljit Nagra,
Maurice Riordan, Jo Shapcott, Laurie Smith and Todd Swift.

And my love to Patrick; and to my family, especially my brother Michael.

ARTS COUNCIL
ENGLAND
Supported using public funding by

The author acknowledges the assistance of Arts Council England,
which made a grant available to enable the completion of this collection.

Contents

Camelament   7

Before the Match   8

Afflatus in My Home Town   9

Leaving Glawdom by night—   11

Violette, Michaela et al, according to Mildred   13

My Mother, the Monsoon   15

When we awake   16

Declare   17

For Our Extinguished Guests   18

redress   20

UNDERLAND   21

a young woman undressed me and   22

Love Cow   23

RILT   25

EDWARDIANA   26

Brother   27

Three Young Surrealist Women…   28

In Bushy Park   29

T-E-N-G-U   30

Bus to Piura   32

His Wife in the Corner   33

The Retirement of Madame Poulay   34

Camelament

Whistle, *chica*,
whist. Give your ear
close and flutter. And flutter.
Eat in all you can hear.
Grow rotund on it, fit
as a fiddler's wife's
cat. There are other kinds
of right learning. Cause
you know. Cause you hear.
Bilge goes out with the suds.
A chain of Cheyennes
touches the lodge of
an enemy. You explode
flat on the floor. Fat
on fear. Flayed
with sharp and hot, and not.

Before the Match

William lets me wear her ring—
a good brother, our two hearts caudate
and sheepshanked since babyhood.

A grab of gold and emerald
I take it to bed with me and stare at it
by candlelight till the sheen lures me in

and I figure in the greeny-yellow lick
her leaf-mould eyes—her thin waist—
her black rope of hair caught

like a noose on the neck
of an errant stallion—
her bell-voice calling out to

Billy, Billy, for help, but he's stepped aside
to visit with me and is saying, *Dear Sis,
things will be as they were.*

His voice, my own tones back to me,
freezes my *sang-froid;* cauterises
bobbing girl-gladness.

I put her back in the flame's eye
twenty-one times more, murmuring. I tell him
I had a dream and he lifts his soft face to me.

Afflatus in My Home Town

I eat. I eat perflux and paper flying
sideways in the dust. I pull soft

conversations from the bones of old men,
jawing at bus stops, about horses' form

and ale. Small girls look broken and mended
wrong. I lick them over. I cannot believe

I have been mute here so long, in these grand
avenues, under this low flat wind, where

everything is old—*the old school, the old post office,
the old library*, all turned to high-end shells.

We are living like wraiths. Women fixed in flux
so familiar it's stasis, black eyes accepting

nothing, marital breath sour and agonal.
We hold wrong in our fists. Wasted,

I look for food, some viaticum
to get me home. Paper and perflux ingested

for no more than jesting, party-words
passed round like canapés when we should scream

or else keep silence so extreme it might be counted
as currency to buy us out.

Our people are eating bitter palliatives,
in a bound world. And where breath should blow

in churches, it's kept in check
in tomes, by those who treasure thrift

and handle special keys. The breath rattles
tabernacle doors, coughing between leaves

while thin lips importune us. The dead,
too, accompany us, uncomprehending

of worsted blankets which we hunch
around our ears when we are wronged,

worsted by circumstance. I can scarcely
believe I have been silent this far. Imbricated

in psychic architecture, like a snail
carrying sweet freight, bent on inching flight.

I mimic enjoyment, *jouissance*,
thrill-less sin—my ego an *outré* gent

gaunt with pleasure, opal-strung: he kisses me
slow with garlic tongue and rubbish

skill. Till I become perflux, paper shifting
and oil-stained, in alien hands.

Leaving Glawdom by night—

dressed glam in twisted serpent
bangles and a sly mothy stole
I set off north by north-east
for seven leagues until I met

the sea, arching Atlantic
coastline, white foam, high noise
and 3 youths, smiling, yelling
into the wind, selling

apples, peddling riddles.
I asked them how many years—
did they know—they called back
dozens; how far out to sea—

America; where the treasure
was—*in silver conches hanging
from the wreck which pirates
ransacked last November.*

I thanked them, pretending
to understand, and bought 3 russets,
rough and tawny, slid them
inside my knapsack and continued

south by south-west for thirteen
furlongs until I met
an old forest creaking
with gold and auburn baubles—

humming birds attending—
and squirrels swivelling rich trinkets
until the branches seemed to dance
and I thought I understood

and glanced around for maidens
I could quiz, but there were none
and I shrugged off my bag,
kicked loose my sandals, gripped moss

between my toes and smelled
woodsmoke, half-baked apples, saw
the whole darn forest
tonguing devilish

orange flames and I tried
to plot the hopping curlicue
edges with my pencil and my
compass and where were

those mystic maidens who could guide
and give me wisdom and suddenly
I heard them laughing, high-stepping
in a glade, they were rifling

plated conches full of treasure
dangling bracelets from their teeth
jewels banging on their chins
and I looked aghast—me a ghost

half-rubicund and silt with ash—
what could I ask?

Violette, Michaela et al, according to Mildred

What if it were all
an accident of alliteration
a serendipity of pinned-down sound?
   [Letter from Mildred's penfriend, early September]

Violette

is cooled in a cocked hat, played to by viols in a lock-in at Ryan's
Bar. She's a shivery walk on the strand at dawn with no sleeping,
muck-tired, swaddled in a plaid blanket, a chieftain's sidekick.
Film-makers set up a nostalgic scene at the beach graveyard,
snaffling ideas from the real funeral on Tuesday. The same leather
coat and Celtic cross. For the 'film funeral', the tide is a creased
Galway shawl in the background and the double-bed grave of
the couple who would not be parted is foreground. Brief blarting
of 'Danny Boy'. She piles her hair up in October till they say she
looks like a spring chicken. Lucky.

Michaela

is ten roubles for a gulag hotel, sharp and solitary as a *poustinia*.
She speaks no words before noon, and until twilight only
mumbles in lisping Spanish to her canary-lookalike parrot. He
answers her in precise Old English and is critical. She dries her
scrubbing brushes on the back step, leaves washing stretched
over bushes in the clearing. Makes foot salve with fresh sage, for
the days are long, and not long.

Valerie

is a collection of bird books, ragged at the edges, and marked
with guano. She is especially volume 2, pages 69, Guillemot, and
70, Kittiwake. Her father is Kite, Birds of Prey, the returners, p.
83, and her mother, Blackbird, British Favourites (p. 100 and
frontispiece). Her brother, Robin, is insouciant, head of the
gang, with a brutish mating call.

Emily

is mapped onto shifting sand, her margins leaky and capricious.
Each square of the grid deceptive, smoked. When the tide is out,
the flats gleam like wet dog belly and look luscious to bury your
nose into and inhale.

Postscript

I stopped askew and looked for you,
blessings strewn like litmus paper after
an alkaline experiment... Along the
hunting halls, lewd trophies of gross-
jowled reindeer, gorgons of sense,
multi-layered rat-catchers of desire:
Plantagenet surprise gives way to rued
Tudor delight.

*[Postcard from Mildred to her
penfriend, late August]*

My Mother, the Monsoon

I go out early to do her messages, to avoid her brylcreemed exes who will dip in at the bookies, betting on snow for Christmas, rain on St Swithin's Day. And her brigade of lady-friends who breakfast, who finger meaty garnets at their throats and linger over each other's wrinkles, ogling. The comedy of correctness. Back home, the house is full of ticks; of mad cousins making money, breaking culture with karate chops, gnawing on it with their eyeteeth. Moderation is one over the top for the mother. Who is family for the old lady dwindling, circled by doctors and district nurses like the farmer's wife in her den? The beautiful and the stunned. I'm suddenly dumped into a whole year of mouldy Mondays, arcane and off the boil. Be still for the postman, lick his lovely thumb. Dumb-lovely, plump with packages. If you are good he will give you a neighbour's missive. It's not considered dishonest any more, he says, he has a dispensation and is probably double-jointed. This family is a becalmed army, idiot with sealed passion. Mother has climate change for a personality. I have become one of the draughts in a stately home, brocade-curtained and visited nostalgically. Don't take me for lost. I have cleaned the carpet of every room with my rasping tongue, rinsed each with tears. Don't take me for the host. Be sick, she says, it's less risky and you'd make a lovely corpse, chisel-cheeked, and modest. She rains for half my life.

When we awake

Four men at the bedside of a loved one. One moves forward roughly—there is always one who has some thought, some shooting-up of emotion which he has bent back like steel, but whose springing forward into this curtained, candled closet of a room he cannot suppress (it is inevitable). A scuffle: voices raised and pulled down again, like foxes trying to escape over a fence. I speak a prayer and wake.

You are not here. Your footprints on the step would have been talisman against such terrors. I drift back. In the dream-room, the eldest brother—it is so obvious that they are brothers, the Slavic cheekbones, the gold-red hair—is livid, his face reflecting rays off the tucked-in body on the bed, whose carefully splayed limbs wait under the sheet, as if in anticipation of death-as-masseur. His eyes hook the younger brothers' eyes in a kind of hateful crochet. Murderous words like 'inheritance' hop in the static. The moon nudges in at the sash, open to gossip, eager to infiltrate moon-logic into this fetid manhole. One brother snatches the curtain and secures it. I am praying again, involuntarily, the words tripping over each other like voyeurs pushing forward after an accident, the room rocking like a mad cradle.

Daylight. Curtains ripped open to reveal an icy but sun-hung morning, running with spring juices. In my room, fresh clutter—boots, a Bible, four men's jackets—relaxes into the general pile. Reek of candle-grease. My neck creaks, arms and legs need to be rubbed to life. I hear singing from below, a spindly strain circles the balcony. When we awake it will be like this.

Declare

In the *clair* of the morning, a streaky-bacon sky, unkosher dawn,
me tumbling to prayer, still at the unclean edges of it, my
morning-self dipped below the surface, just starting to steep, the
first psalm half-unravelled, when

the wedge of the attic fills full-tilt with an impatient important
egg-yolk wash, water sucked through a plug, backwards. And
two-thirds of the way into the room, at the golden section, an
ivory figure with forearms extended, bristling

with razor-rays and a curious asking asking. Two ivory fists in
front of my face—'right or left?' he quizzes me, me wordless fool
of a girl opening opening. He flips a fist to reveal a golden sliver,
a lip, a pip he plants in me

like pre-flesh, a shiver of ice to steal my breath, bind up my
yesses and noes. A seed word, syllable, choking over and over,
promising to tell tight salt things I want to shut my ears to. Then
me hotfoot to Elizabeth, skimming

rough hillsides like a ducks-and-drakes pebble, the syllable gut-
tering over and over, me trying to outpace it. And then E! rubicund,
humble puffed-out and plumped wineskin, replete. And the pip
shaking me

to bless her, to sport with her child, the two of us mothers circled
in a hoary girdle, like a cat's cradle, blushing at each other, our
bellies brought into contact, kissing, me sensing the rough spurt
of the one who is before the one he is to go before

For Our Extinguished Guests

I
So Mother Abbess delays a few days in the selva,
adventures alongside the laity
in toucan-touched rainforests, tickled
by tigerlight striping her habit. She turns *frissonista*
at the thought of real terrorists laired up with jaguars
and monkeys; brushes breasts against *copaiba,*
pretty *malva,* thick-set cedar. Steers the tour-guide
past poisonous pencil snakes, then strikes out
for her own territory, the desert, and slick
monastic gig she runs on the skirts
of a shanty-town, at the edge
of a tip, rubbing shoulders with rubbish.
Presents her travelling companion—

II
The father, clicked into guest-quarters,
is corn-fed and watered by pale nuns who
come and go with purple *morada,* iced lemon,
and a yard broom to keep the steps clear
of sand; their eyes dart low, bright blue. He thirsts
for his arum-lily, his daughter
transplanted, imagines her
growing twisted, amongst similar.
He asks questions, raises eyebrows
in Spanish, flicks copper roaches
from pillows. Ticks off gold mornings
throbbing with scarlet-tongued flowers. Activities
are arranged: the beach; Museum of the Sea. He glimpses her
three times a day through the grille.

III
The daughter, inside the enclosure, dreams
of peacocks and snow. Rises earlier, collides
with a junta of nuns who, as if playing chess, devise
urgent sweeping, singing, and scaling of fish;
keep her busy. No visits. His ticket expires.

Ceremonial farewells: they hug;
she smuggles a shell to her mother
(*give nothing unless the Abbess allow*);
then watches planes, which might be his,
arc the desert—the selva of paired birds,
painted rainforests, terrorists—the mountains—away—

Soon after, she breaches the cloister-wall; arcs the desert-and-
                                        selva-and-
mountains herself; returns to her father, November, fireworks like
gunshots, brief birds climbing the night, and the original wall
made of muscle and will.

redress

after Carolyn Forché

(I don't lift my sweater I don't show you
but where hair billows like tangleweed

a teal vein pulses)

        I hitch my skirt   above where the knee is
        scraped

        your skin is crushed walnuts your hair spilt
        orange paint
        your eyes iron oxide smeared over screwed-up
        to-do lists

the torn moon hangs on, by a thread
Glory be, says the mother—what you been doing in the blackberries,
Missy. Your legs are—
                I let hot jersey cover the mottle and burn

there's rebel whistling between my teeth
as she holds slate to my face
picks a knife to prick her initials
into my jaw her breath
like reheated beans
as she tallies my sins
               listens to the news later
               her expert hands shaving flowers
               for the feast—flying

UNDERLAND

(after that man 'Lewis')

Towards winter solstice, Alice
can no longer cope with groping down blind alleys,
being groped by creatures she doesn't
comprehend, in places obscure
to her. She has issues
with size, this human yoyo, no permanence and issues
between her thighs, no liniments. No
malice. Just a sweet intrinsic *no*
to everything. A refusal
to go along. This long winternight
is ritual to her, good rich black
fostering. Freedom
from his wittering.

a young woman undressed me and

five minutes later she undressed me again
ten minutes after that she undressed me
and again fifteen minutes later
by which time I was beginning to feel tender
her fingers were cool and her palms firm
as she disembarrassed me of one hot layer
after another, tweed, cotton, nylon, loosing
buttons and cuffs, unravelling ties—

when she had been undressing me for a month
I dared to say, sideways, my mouth under the chest
of a pullover which she was easing over my head
with such skill and love that my adams apple
felt like it had been rolled in honey
and rubbed in oats, and my voice was grungy
and low, my skin somewhat shiny
and raw: *muhuuhu muhuuhu ph ph ph hmmhu hm*—
she touched my lip with a shapely thumb—
shhh, don't fret. her voice like jinxed june breezes
in lime leaves. and then. her voice like rills rushing over flint
and dazzling in sunlight. we'll get you undressed and then
we'll see to that. just a moment now. and still
she continues to undress me

Love Cow

Oh cow of love you have me pinned
to your evergreen felt

and are in at my ear with fermenting
oaths and actual importuning

and imprecations. I rebut you
with a tough raft of arguments, derived

from magazines under the sofa
at my Aunt Libbie's house

I have a disease, your rump is small,
your rich cream disgusts me

and others which are more
sophisticated, from the Bible and books of

philosophy. You give me a soft brown
stare. How I wobble now before you, cow

of love, humongous, like a free-range
sack of boulders swaying

delightfully, your cordial spine
rippling, your celtic skeleton

offering promise. To eat you
would be divine, surely,

your emerald milk fast-forwarding
to your stomachs, pressed over and over

by clenching muscles. Why is it you cows get
such bad press? I wonder, half-beguiled.

Sometimes I see you, fenced,
defending young ('let go of your dog

if cows surround you', the notice
on the farm gate says)

or at the abattoir, steaming hot
and hung prosaically on hooks.

Or on the plate with no relief
except for some mocking green

salad—staked out, defenceless.
They say your flesh can stay

unsullied in the gut
for six months or more—

bowels fill with longing
for sloping fields, a faraway sea.

RILT

Perturbée, like the best of them,
I manoeuvred my way to the edge,
took the half-sunned shallows of puddles
in the cut as my birthright. 'I have,'
I said, 'a right to walk this way.'
I looked round, smite-faced, at the other
crooked-leg girls like me, proud.

'But go back,' I said to my companion
who like me had the mid-blue wavering
eyes, 'and ask them if it's allowed for us
girls to climb the velvety brow of the hill,
cross the common and go down
all the way to the sea.'

EDWARDIANA

An inch or two skimmed from her twill skirt
and the day shaped perfectly in her head:
seamless tennis, swimming, a cycle down the lane
and up, a rondeau of elevenses with aunts,

then two loops unhooked from her corset
for patriotic postprandial singing round the piano,
the map of England shaved perfectly on her head.

Strong tea in thin-lipped china, a cakestand charged
with madeleines and buttered teabreads—mountains!—
shared perfectly by her bed: a long ramble
with a newish lover, in slant-lit gardens, mallow

weighting the air and, under row after row
of high-arching yew, yards and yards
of shadow waiting perfectly up ahead.

Brother

Not the physical boy but the masculine
shadow, cruciform over the family, fixed from
eldest to youngest, sprinting alongside as well
as over us, quick to fill our mouths to stop us
from mentioning his name, leapfrogging into
the space where joy was, long-jumping through
the marrow, where his disease had been—and
we were death-struck, dumb, not realising he
only wanted to play.

Three Young Surrealist Women Holding in their Arms the Skins of an Orchestra, 1936 — Dalí

Having always used her music as an instrument, a gift to stifle hurt in others, a searching for a niche into which she could stuff pansies or wallflowers, a grey to be drenched with peony or tangerine, she became pliable, perfectly responsive to circumstance, a kitten following its master, chase-and-nibble. At first she didn't notice herself changing, so intent was she on pacifying with titbits the yawning jaw. Filling the jug of subjugation. Until she awoke in a boulder-desert, stone-faced, immaterial. Her life shrunk now to two needers who dominated: her mother and her daughter. Her music no more than a cipher, a distorted keyboard painted on a banner wrung out, flung out between her and the others, a mute offering. The godlike gift something less than animal or vegetable. A split skewed thing. And she, a rock-musician, no longer able to please anyone.

In Bushy Park

I am in Bushy Park with flies. Don't leave me, causing a stink, trampling my ideas like *aspergillus* rolled round in leaf-rot. A cardboardy crust encases the pie we bought—a classic roast pastified for ramblers—which we eat like wolves. We count six goatees of sheep's wool, wizened trophies strung on a gate. I like the look of your white white. *Mazel tov.* Monsieur, when I started this walk I had three clear objectives. You trounced the first, and the others, though half-engaged, were seduced by a boy with tweedy jacket and bolt-upright glance. No, Lord, too sad. I seven times circled the station saying prayers like the handbook had told me, trying to shut out the noise of aeroplanes and day-trippers. A goodly mardikin of pomegranates and Russian vodkas airy as voile, meshed with steel, wait back at the hostel. Slip your hand in mine, Monsieur, keep me in mind while we traverse this last field with the delicious dip demented with daisies. I had a thought a while back, when we were clambering the stone wall, unsnagging ourselves from doubled barbed wire, what it would be like to meet you half-way, your prejudices porous with travel and age, your eyes on the pearl. I take a step back, find a footing that feels hopeful, gazellate myself onto a nearby boulder, pyramid, above marsh. Feel *between,* trapezeless. How can you stay so solid, *ambulator grande*, like a colonel, while I hop and spit, wobble and use all my skill to stay still. An arm of a damsel reaches out from the mire and I've half a mind to pull her in, though the three of us turning up late won't go down well. Catch as catch can, blow up the Empire State Building and still order your thoughts, like huskies in training, all pulling as one. And then in a moment, it's over, a dog grabs and snaps her delicate arm to the elbow, her eyes are grey and unfocused as she turns round to me with a will, with a *why?*

T-E-N-G-U*

Tender as ten good men, but sword-chewing and tenser. The temple guard salutes you, though his temple is suburbia with a run of garages to house your noses like red phalluses—lousephilanthropist-

louse—all the way down the street. Mackerel-fearing, fond of flambé, you're a card and a harpy and a heavenly dogg-ess. Comet. Kite. In Japanese, *Ten-gu*. In Osaka, in a cracked-open garden at dawn—

red cranes screaming in maple—and a gem of a girl found lost, stencilled with blood, gleaming at men who'd stripped the place to find her, garnet heart tearing up tarmac, swearing at sky. One man found a nest of eggs,

sweet as a peahen's, but poison to those of shorn tongue. Tengu—in Anglo-Saxon, Tengu. In letters, Renga; in South American dance, merengue, tango. Maybe I'll let go of her in verse, the shrew, her grab-ready hands

and her pinched chin, her volley of quick-picked cavils, jabbed from needle-tongue. Sleep-sparing, night-flying daybird, I'll disembarrass her. Her face always close to mine, reading my thoughts.

I'll loose her. Like in a lucid dream, I'll imagine I'm gifted to rinse myself in citronella, shake my shoulders and head for the shore. In Chinese, Den-gu. In nursery English, Ten-

gooey. In primary-based colours, tangerine. In prime numbers, ten-minus-3-gu; in Kazakhstan currency, tengeh. Peremptory priestess, you hold your own service at the foot of the mountain face cut from red sofa-leather, plush, you have ten million waiting, but you look like you've forgotten the words, you stir up a typhoon with your feather-fan and it fills your robes with thunder and your nose drips, the heart you had

views your body's machinery from a distance, can't sleep on gold, curls away from the light, you trickable spirit, you latcher, you lame apostrophe to an Old Master.

Your nasal singing—tone glue—rends the temple—trends queue —tends to—dense-cool—men who—trapped you—Zen crew.

In Australian, Ken-do. In Betweenheavenandhell, *Tengu*.

*Mythical Japanese flying creature, associated with spirits of priests and nuns, neither damned nor blessed, offering false images of the Buddha, typically long-nosed, and reputed to dislike the smell of mackerel...

Bus to Piura

We, white-habited *madrecitas,*
our veils snapping in the desert wind, waiting
for a bus to the *monasterio,* are snared
by a bright rabble of staring kids—
jet-haired, ponchoed—

who have us circled in a moment,
arms folded, drinking us in,
our oyster skin, our sea-coloured eyes.
We wriggle. They gasp.
We blush, become television.

His Wife in the Corner

When he had finished offering me the world
and stretched up to switch on the light
and looked back with a curious green glow
in his eyes—his cheeks plumped out and young-looking—
at his handiwork, me lying there replete,
a jetted calf, pinioned, a vodka bottle
nodding in the hollow between us
like it had some fang-dang urgent message,

I felt like I was 14 and had raced in my lunch hour
to the store with the jade velvet jacket in the window,
carried on a wave of longing and with all the confidence
of sudden money, only to be met in the lobby by the assistant
in civvies, saying 'we don't open on Tuesdays'
and his wife in the corner dressed sharp and rocking violently,
her gorgeous green lapels rising and falling with mirth.

The Retirement of Madame Poulay

When she had outgrown being a beauty, she flipped
to being ugly and found it a lot less wearing.

No files of men with rasping beards insistent
at the stage door with their rat-a-tat-tats.

No sighs on the phone. No battling
for a room's space, an hour's peace.

No tyrannous *régime* at the barre—no blenching
of rouge—exfoliating heels till they bled—abstaining

from bread and fat—channelling a beatific smile.
No costly gowns allowed, but—*sacré bleu*—the luxury

of lying low like a cow come home, absolved
from chit-chat, those worn-out, trotted-out tropes

(*'comme ci, comme ça'*). With powdered hair unravelling
down her back, she tastes *déshabillée* the bliss of being

unknown, a common crone who has the livelong day
to play, to pick out crazy baby dance-steps

of her own.

www.ingramcontent.com/pod-product-compliance
Lightning Source LLC
Chambersburg PA
CBHW021947040426
42448CB00008B/1279